Marvels of Creation

Magnificent Mammals

BUDDY & KAY DAVIS

Marvels of Creation
Magnificent Mammals

Second Printing, May 2008

Previously published as *Special Wonders of the Wild Kingdom*.

ISBN: 0-89051-456-9
Library of Congress: 2005907663

For other great titles visit our website:
www.masterbooks.net

For information regarding author interviews, please contact the publicity department at (870) 438-5288.

PRINTED IN CHINA

Master Books
A Division of New Leaf Publishing Group
www.masterbooks.net

Acknowledgments

Writing a book is a team effort, and we have the best team anyone could ask for: the Answers in Genesis staff. Special thanks go to Brandon Vallorani and Dan Zordel for their hard work and dedication to this project.

— Buddy & Kay Davis

Contents

Introduction

It seems that no matter what book about wildlife we read, God isn't even mentioned. Wildlife programs are full of indoctrination in evolution. This book erases all evolutionary concepts and gives God the glory for His creation.

This is a collection of some unique and wonderful animals that God created. Its purpose is to give you information on each animal and the special way that God designed each one.

Some of the animal design features that appear to be dangerous are a result of the fall caused by Adam's rebellion in the Garden of Eden. Sin affected the whole world and all creation groans because of it (Rom. 8:22). Thorns and thistles started to grow. It was probably during this time that some of the animals changed and became aggressive in their behavior. The Bible also tells us that animals began to fear man after the global flood of Noah's day (Gen. 9:2).

God promises a time is coming when the wolf will lie down with the lamb and the lion will eat straw as an ox (Isa. 11:6–7). We look forward to that time. Until then, we can worship God and marvel at the special wonders of the wild kingdom.

The complexities of life and the design implied therein are strong monuments to a Creator and the

Genesis account of creation upon which mankind can build a strong defense for faith in God.

On the other hand, those same complexities expose evolution as an outdated theory with many flaws. For how could time, matter, and chance ever create life out of nothing? Even for the simplest of life forms to exist would require thousands of complex molecules to form at the same instant, precisely integrated with each other, carrying massive amounts of information.

For more complex forms to keep evolving would require large numbers of favorable mutations to continually add new information. However, the probability of many complex, interacting, information-bearing molecules all forming at the same time is zero, and science has so far not even observed one mutation that adds new information. In fact, nearly all mutations are either neutral or harmful, not favorable or beneficial. Even those rare ones that are a benefit degrade the information; i.e., they are "useful defects."

In addition, the complexities of life reach a level beyond any "natural" explanation, for DNA, the information system in all living cells, is useless without another information system already in place to read, understand, and act upon it. Evolutionists teach that DNA is a product of chance, but how do they explain the system that interprets it? The truth is, there is no explanation because information must always come from information, which must ultimately come from a source of intelligence, and that source of intelligence must ultimately be an infinite Intelligence.

This complexity of life works on another scale as well: the interaction of complex mechanisms. Living things are full of complicated systems and structures, especially at the microscopic level, which would be useless unless all of the components were there at once. Even supposing that the information required for life and the complexities of interacting systems did arise by chance, evolution still lacks the fossil evidence that such transitional steps occurred. Charles Darwin admitted that the fossil record lacked this evidence, but he believed that the transitional forms would be found in time. However, after 140 years, the only evidence scientists have found in the rock layers supports the abrupt appearance of the various animal kinds without any real transitional forms. The oldest fossil dragonfly still looks like a dragonfly. The oldest fossil bat still looks like a bat. The oldest fossil fish still looks like a fish. And the list goes on and on. Evolution still has the same problem with the fossil record that Darwin noted, yet the sudden appearance of all the different kinds of plants and animals is exactly what we would expect to find

if creation were true. The fossil record supports the evidence of God's created kinds and the destruction of most of that creation by a worldwide flood.

Even without transitional forms, evolutionists explain that some animals look similar because they must be related and have a common ancestor. For example, the skeleton of a cow shows similarities in structure to the skeleton of a bear. This homology, they explain, is proof of evolution. But it would have been logical for God, in His infinite wisdom, to use a common design, or basic plan, when He created everything. It is readily apparent that a house or factory or skyscraper are all different and specially designed. Yet they all have similarities in their structure, such as a foundation, walls, roof, doors, windows, plumbing, electrical wires, and so on. And the thought of such a building constructing itself by chance over millions of years is ridiculous, yet even one living cell is more complex in structure and chemical make-up than the most detailed building mankind could ever build.

The marvelous design and complexity of life speak boldly of the Creator God's infinite wisdom in creating the wondrous animals that populate the earth. One example of God's ultimate wisdom is the giraffe. The giraffe's neck, made up of the same seven bones that all mammals possess in their necks, yet accounting for nearly half the animal's total height, is neither too rigid nor too flexible. Fewer joints would reduce the amount of muscles required to hold the head aloft, but increase breakability of the neck. More joints would increase flexibility of the neck but increase muscle weight, which would upset the giraffe's center of balance. To accommodate its long neck, the giraffe possesses larger than normal lungs that pump air at a slower rate to accommote its ten-foot (3 m) trachea, reinforced artery walls in the brain to prevent them from bursting due to the sudden pressure increase when the animal bends to drink, and special capillaries that prevent blood pooling and profuse bleeding in the legs.

The giraffe also must give birth standing up, and the baby is uniquely delivered to prevent breaking the neck: the hind feet exit first to break the baby's fall and the neck is bent to the side with the head cushioned on its rear hips as it passes through the birth canal. Truly, the Creator's wisdom has produced an animal uniquely designed to fill a special niche.

When scientists first examined a specimen of the platypus, they thought it was made up of pieces of different animals put together: a taxidermist's hoax. However, all of the pieces of this unique little animal from Australia were specially designed by a wise Creator. Some of the amazing characteristics of the platypus include webbed feet, a beaver-like tail, and poisonous spurs on the hind legs of the males. The platypus lays eggs much like a lizard, but nurses its young from milk glands. In addition, the platypus has a leathery bill that contains sensitive receptors that are able to pick up electric signals. The platypus uses this bill instead of its eyes to search for food under the water. Truly a marvelously designed animal, the platypus defies evolutionary explanation.

The list of creatures evidencing such wondrous design and complexity is not just a testament to the creative hand of the supreme God, but also a living reminder of His curse because of sin.

The Bible tells us that when God finished His creation on the sixth day, everything was very good (Gen. 1:24–25). We also know from Scripture that all animals were once vegetarians and lived together in peace (Gen. 1:31–2:1). From this description, we know that we do not live in the same world that God originally created, being witnesses to the fact that there is much disease, death, and suffering. We now see animals eating other animals, inherited mutational mistakes, and inbreeding causing disease and deformity, and a growing list of endangered and extinct species. Because of Adam's disobedience in the Garden of Eden, all of creation groans in pain (Rom. 8:22).

American Bison

Also known as the buffalo, millions of American bison once roamed across the American plains. Native Americans depended on bison for their food and clothing, and used the dung — called buffalo chips — as fuel for their fires.

The coat of the bison is dark brown. It is very shaggy at the shoulders, actually consisting of two layers. A thick undercoat traps body warmth. The outer coat, which is shed in the summer, is made of long guard hairs that keep out wind and shed water. The hump on a bison's back consists of muscle and bone used to support the buffalo's large head. Both the male and the female have curved horns.

Bison do not have good eyesight, but they have a sharp sense of smell and very good hearing. They can maintain speeds up to 35 miles (56 km) per hour for as long as a half-hour, and are also excellent swimmers.

Bison are migratory grazers. Their food is chewed, then swallowed and regurgitated. This is called chewing the cud, but the scientific name is rumination. Like all bovines, the bison does not have any incisors in the roof of its mouth, but it does have a pad and jaw teeth.

Although bison look like overgrown cattle, they are wild animals and can be extremely dangerous. During the breeding season, the bulls are easily provoked, and a cow with a calf will protect it by charging. On the other hand, when a herd feels threatened, the cows will surround the calves, and the bulls will surround the cows.

Adult bison have few enemies, though wolves and coyotes may attack the old, sick, or young. Females mature in two to four years, usually producing one calf per breeding season — July through September. After a gestation period of nine months, calves weigh about 65 pounds (29 kg) when born and are able to stand in a couple of hours.

Early American settlers nearly wiped out the buffalo, reducing the bison population from over 50 million to around 500. After they were put on the endangered species list, the herds increased to over 100,000 bison by 1991.

Today, farms and ranches raise bison for their meat and hide. Because bison and domestic cattle are of the same kind (Bovidae), they can reproduce and their offspring are called "beefalos." Since bison are very territorial and prefer to stay close to their home range, they are hard to contain in new surroundings. Farmers usually purchase calves because mature bison will break through the sturdiest of fences to return to their original home.

American Bison

ARTIODACTYLA • BOVIDAE • BISON BISON

HEIGHT: 6 feet (1.8 m) at the shoulder

WEIGHT: 2,210 pounds (1,000 kg)

LENGTH: 12 feet (3.7 m) from head to tail.

Life Span: 20 years in the wild, up to 40 years in captivity.

SPECIAL DESIGN FEATURE: The coat of the bison is actually two coats. One is a thick undercoat to trap body warmth and the other has long guard hairs to keep out the wind and it sheds water.

DID YOU KNOW? The American bison is the largest land mammal on the American continent.

Bactrian Camel

The Bactrian camel is the only truly wild, two-humped camel in the world. It is named for the area it inhabits, Bactria, on the border of the former Soviet Union. The wild camel once roamed all of Asia but now can only be found in the Gobi Desert.

Special God-designed features of the camel make survival in the harsh desert possible. It has thick, wooly fleece to protect it from the hot sun and help it fight off the cold in the winter; the wool is dark brown to beige. The camel can tolerate great variations in temperature. Other special features include nostrils that close to keep the sand out, eyelashes that are double-rowed to protect the eyes, knees that are padded for kneeling, and broad feet with expandable pads for walking in the sand.

The Bactrian camel feeds on tough grass, herbs, branches, shrubs, and foliage. They have a four-chambered stomach and chew their cud like a cow. They usually search for food in the early morning or evening.

One amazing feature of this camel is its two humps. These humps are food and water reserves. The camel can go a long time without water (up to ten times longer than man can), and can drink up to 125 pints (237 l) to replenish its water supply.

The Bactrian camel herds contain 6 to 20 animals led by a mature male. These camels breed in February, and their gestation period lasts 13 months. Within several days of birth, the calf can keep up with its mother very well. The calf will nurse for five years, at which point it reaches maturity.

Man has domesticated some Bactrian camels. They are an important resource for wool, milk, meat, and transportation in the desert.

Bactrian Camel

ARTIODACTYLA • CAMELIDAE • CAMELUS BACTRIANUS

HEIGHT: 6 feet (1.8 m)

LENGTH: 10 feet (3 m)

WEIGHT: 1,575 pounds (700 kg)

LIFE SPAN: longest recorded, 50 years

SPECIAL DESIGN FEATURE: The wool of the camel protects it from extreme weather, its nostrils close to keep sand out, and their broad feet expand to walk easily in the sand.

DID YOU KNOW? The fat in the humps of the camel store reserves of food and water. They can survive ten times longer than man can without water.

Beaver

Busy as a beaver is a term nearly everyone has heard. It's easy to see where the saying comes from, for the beaver is always working, whether it is chopping down trees, repairing its home, or gathering food for the winter. The largest rodent in North America, the beaver has chestnut-brown fur and a dark gray, paddle-shaped, scaly tail which it uses as a rudder when swimming. Beavers also use their tails as warning devices, slapping them on the water to warn other beavers of danger. The beaver also has strong, bright orange front teeth, which are used to cut down trees and trim branches.

A beaver likes to build its home in the middle of a pond. Sometimes these homes have two or more entrances. They cut down trees on both sides of the stream and sometimes transport them by constructing a canal upon which the trees float to the pond.

Beavers build watertight dams out of logs, branches, mud, and small rocks, thereby diverting streams and creating ponds. These dams vary in size and can be several hundred yards long by as much as 12 feet (3.6 m) high. A beaver will work all of its life to maintain a dam. Engineers are amazed at the efficiency and effectiveness of the design of beaver dams.

Beavers live in large, stable family groups consisting of one adult pair, their newborn young, and the young born the previous year. Beavers mate for life and breed during the winter. Baby beavers, called kits, are born in the spring. A litter can have as many as eight kits. They stay in the home pond until they are about two years old.

Early settlers of North America hunted the beaver for its valuable fur and for meat. The population of beavers declined dramatically until regulations and careful planning increased their numbers. Although some people regard beavers as nuisances, they actually help prevent soil erosion, create marshlands, and construct a complicated system of dams and canals that regulate flooding.

Beaver

RODENTIA • CASTORIDAE • CASTOR CANADENSIS

HEIGHT: 12–24 inches (30–61 cm)

WEIGHT: 25–55 pounds (11–25 kg)

LENGTH: 24–32 inches (61–81 cm)

LIFE SPAN: 15 to 20 years

SPECIAL DESIGN FEATURE: The beaver has amazed engineers with their effectiveness of design in building their homes and dams.

DID YOU KNOW? The beaver is the largest rodent in North America.

Black Rhinoceros

The black rhinoceros is noted for being ill-tempered and very aggressive, often charging for no apparent reason. Although normally slow moving, the rhino can charge at an alarming rate of speed, and it can easily kill whatever it hits with its deadly pointed horns. The horn is made up of matted hair, and poachers market it as a medicine.

The black rhino is easily distinguished from its white cousin because it is shorter and has a smaller head and ears. It also has a uniquely long and pointed upper lip, which it uses to gather leaves, acacia bark, and shoots. Its keen sense of smell and hearing make up for its weak eyes.

The male weighs up to one ton (907 kg); the female is usually smaller. Rhinos have two and sometimes three horns. Black rhinos are browsers that seldom graze. They feed in the early morning and late afternoon.

Rhinos live in bush country, grasslands, and open forests. They have paths throughout their territories that normally include one or two watering holes. They love to wallow in the mud to keep cool, and to protect their skin from the sun and insects.

The breeding season is all year with a gestation period of 18 months. The female rhinos normally bear a single offspring, which can weigh 77 to 88 pounds (35–40 kg) at birth. Newborn rhinos are up and walking within three hours and are weaned at about two years of age. Babies are born when there is plenty of food for the mother, insuring good nourishment for the young. The males are solitary, and the females usually keep their young with them.

Man is the most serious threat to the existence of the black rhinoceros. The rhino has been hunted almost to extinction for its horn.

Black Rhinoceros

PERISSODACTYLA • RHINOCEROTIDAE
DICEROS BICORNIS
HEIGHT: 5 feet (1.6 m)
WEIGHT: 1 ton (907 kg)
LENGTH: 11 feet (3.4 m)
LIFE SPAN: 45 years
SPECIAL DESIGN FEATURE: The black rhinoceros has a very keen sense of smell and hearing.
DID YOU KNOW? The horn of the black rhinoceros is made up of matted hair.

Cheetah

Streamlined and designed to run, the cheetah is the fastest land animal in the world, reaching speeds up to 70 miles (113 km) per hour for short distances.

The cheetah's legs are long and its shoulders high, giving its back a sweeping look. Black spots cover its body, and two distinct dark lines stripe either side of its face. Unlike other large cats, the cheetah cannot retract its claws. The females are generally smaller than the males.

Cheetahs usually hunt at dusk and dawn, resting during the day. Gazelles are their favorite prey, although they will hunt other hoofed animals. Cheetahs approach their prey by stealth and then surprise them by bursting into a sprint and intercepting quickly. When they hunt in groups, cheetahs can bring down prey larger than themselves.

The cheetah's habitat is in savannas and arid, open grasslands in Arabia, Iran, Turkistan, and south of the Sahara in Africa.

The gestation period of the cheetah is 90 to 95 days. A litter consists of four to five cubs which are 12 inches long (30 cm) at birth and, like other cats, born blind. Their den is located in long grasses or bushes. Cubs are dusty white and begin to develop adult coloration at three months, though their backs and neck will remain white until approximately eight months. They will not be mature enough to raise their own families until they are two or three years old. However, they will go hunting with their mother as early as six weeks.

Cheetahs can be and have been domesticated for about 4,000 years. They are easily tamed and have been used by man as a hunting aid.

It is interesting to note that scientists now claim all cats can be traced back to one (three at most) different cat kinds. Science is catching up with God's Word. In Genesis it says that God created the kinds.

Cheetah

CARNIVORA • FELIDAE • ACINONYX JUBATUS

HEIGHT: 2.3' – 2.8' (70–85 cm)

WEIGHT: 120 to 128 pounds (50 to 59 kg)

LENGTH: body - 4.6 to 5 feet (1.4 to 1.5 m), tail - 24 to 28 inches (60 to 70 cm)

LIFE SPAN: up to 12 years

SPECIAL DESIGN FEATURE: The cheetah is designed to run. Its legs are long and its body streamlined.

DID YOU KNOW? The cheetah is the fastest land animal in the world.

Echidna

The echidna, also known as the spiny anteater, is native to Australia, Tasmania, and southern New Guinea. The echidna is an egg-laying mammal. It looks like a hedgehog but is larger with a short, stubby, hairless tail. Porcupine-like spikes, which can grow to as much as two inches long (5 cm), cover its body. These spikes are yellow with a black tip, and hair grows between them. However, the animal's belly is covered with brown fur.

An echidna has an excellent sense of hearing and smell, but poor eyesight. It runs and climbs well. It buries itself quickly if disturbed and, if the ground is too hard to dig, rolls up, exposing a mass of needle-like spikes. Some females and all males have spears on their ankles, and their feet have five toes.

The echidna lives between rocks and hollows, and feeds during the afternoon, searching for ants and termites. It is believed that the echidna uses its nose to pick up electrical signals from insects. It uses its long, sticky, six-inch (15 cm) tongue to trap its meals, and it has spines on the roof of the mouth to scrape the insects off the tongue. If it has to, an echidna can fast up to a month.

Female echidna usually lay one egg, but on rare occasions lay as many as three. The mother incubates her eggs in a temporary pouch for about ten days. Once the eggs hatch, the babies remain in the pouch until their spikes develop. The mother then places her babies in a burrow and nurses them for about three months. The baby echidna sucks milk, which contains a large amount of hemoglobin, from a tuft of hair on its mother's stomach.

Echidnas have few natural enemies; however, the aborigines do eat them.

Echidna

MONOTREMATA • TACHYGLOSSIDAE
TACHYGLOSSUS ACULEATUS, TSETOSUS,
ZAGLOSSUS BRUIJNI

WEIGHT: 6.5 to 14.5 pounds (3 to 6 kg)

LENGTH: 13.5 to 17.5 inches (35 to 45 cm)

LIFE SPAN: 20 years

SPECIAL DESIGN FEATURE: The echidna incubates their egg in a temporary pouch.

DID YOU KNOW? The echidna has a sticky six-inch (15 cm) tongue that traps insects. On the roof of their mouth there are spines that scrape off the insects.

Elephant

The elephant is the largest living land mammal in the world. An elephant has large bones filled with sponge bone instead of marrow, and pads on its feet that absorb the shock from its heavy weight. Its ears are packed with blood vessels and are fanned to bring down body temperature. Its thick skin is tender, and an elephant rolls in the dust to protect it from the hot sun and insects. Elephants love water and like to bathe daily, spraying their bodies and each other with their trunks. They drink nearly 40 gallons (151 l) of water at a time and can eat as much as 500 pounds (227 kg) of vegetation, consisting of fruit, branches, grass, and other foliage.

The elephant is a gentle animal, but becomes extremely dangerous if angered. They have extraordinary power in their trunks, able to kill with a single blow. With as many as 40,000 muscles, an elephant's trunk ends in a lobe or lip that functions like a finger, allowing the elephant to pick up small objects. An elephant's tusks, used for digging and ripping bark, are actually large protruding incisor teeth that grow throughout the elephant's lifetime. Tusks do not grow back when lost.

Social animals that greet each other if they've been apart, elephants communicate by vocal sounds such as trumpeting and purring. Purring is controlled by sounds in their stomach. They usually purr when out of sight of each other, and if they stop purring, it is a sign of danger.

Elephants travel in small troops, usually led by a dominant female. They can live up to 70 years of age, reaching puberty in their middle teens. After a gestation period of 22 months, a single baby is born. Baby elephants nurse for around two years and stay with their mother until puberty. At that time, young bulls are usually driven from the herd to live alone or in bachelor groups.

There are two kinds of elephants alive today: the African elephant and the Asian elephant. There are reports of a few elephants alive near Nepal that have the characteristics of the extinct mammoth.

The elephant's main enemy is man. Poachers unlawfully kill elephants for the ivory tusks and have endangered this wonderful animal to the point of extinction.

Elephant

PROBOSCIDEA • ELEPHANTIDEA
ELEPHAS MAXIMUS (ASIAN ELEPHANT) OR
LOXODONTA AFRICANA (AFRICAN ELEPHANT)
HEIGHT: 15 feet (4 m) (African)
WEIGHT: 6.6 tons (6,000 kg)
LENGTH: 24.8 feet (7.5 m)
LIFE SPAN: 70 years
SPECIAL DESIGN FEATURE: Elephants have excellent hearing and their ears are also used as cooling units.
DID YOU KNOW? African elephants are the largest living land mammal in the world.

Fruit Bat

The fruit bat, also known as the "flying fox," is one of the largest bats in the world, receiving its name from its fox-like face and large eyes. Unlike most bats, this flying mammal uses its sight rather than echolocation to locate food. Hearing the loud squeals of other bats feeding also helps it locate a food source.

Flying foxes have two claws on the leading edge of their wings and pointed teeth. If we look at the jaws of the fruit bat, it has very sharp teeth. Most people have been taught that this is a design for a carnivorous animal. However, this unique creature is 100 percent vegetarian. Their entire diet consists of blossoms and fruit. When feeding on fruit, they drink the juice and spit out the pulp. Flying foxes have trouble getting into the air if caught on the ground, so they feed on fruit in the trees and will not follow a meal if it drops to the ground. They get their water by skimming over rivers and lakes and thus avoid having to land.

Flying foxes are found in Australia. Living in large colonies, they sometimes congregate by the tens of thousands in swamps, rainforests, and near rivers. They roost by hanging upside-down with their wings wrapped around their bodies and, like most bats, sleep during the day and feed at night. They sometimes fly long distances to obtain food.

Born around October, the baby flying fox is carried by its mother for the first two months, after which it is left behind while she feeds at night. The baby will be on its own after three months of age.

The flying fox plays an important role in the pollination of Australia, and its droppings aid in the distribution of seeds. However, many farmers in Australia are forced to cover their fruit to keep the bats from destroying their orchards.

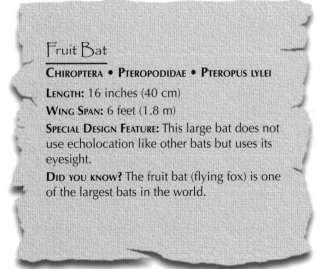

Fruit Bat

CHIROPTERA • PTEROPODIDAE • PTEROPUS LYLEI

LENGTH: 16 inches (40 cm)

WING SPAN: 6 feet (1.8 m)

SPECIAL DESIGN FEATURE: This large bat does not use echolocation like other bats but uses its eyesight.

DID YOU KNOW? The fruit bat (flying fox) is one of the largest bats in the world.

Giant Anteater

The giant anteater with its long, pointed nose is easy to identify. Four species of anteater are found in the open forests and savannas of Central and South America. Along with its elongated nose, its head and neck are tapered, and it has small ears, eyes, and mouth. It does not have any teeth.

The coat of the anteater is coarse and shaggy — short on the head and very long on the silver-white striped back. The front feet of the anteater have five toes, of which the second and third toes are very strong and have long claws. The anteater will actually walk on its knuckles to protect these claws.

Although the anteater cannot see well, it has a very acute sense of smell, up to 40 times more powerful than man's. It uses smell to locate its meals. Its diet is mainly ground-dwelling ants, although it will also eat termites, fruit, and larvae. Anteaters use their strong front feet to open the termite and anthills.

The anteater's tongue has tiny spines that point backward and can stretch two feet (61 cm) down an ant hole. Also, the tongue is covered with a sticky substance that enables the anteater to extract insects quite easily from their hills.

The giant anteater is solitary. In the wild, it forages during the daytime, but if its range is located near a town, it will wait until dark to feed. The giant anteater sleeps up to 15 hours a day, and its body temperature is 89.6 degrees Fahrenheit, which enables it to survive on its diet of ants.

The mating season for the anteater is March to May. After a 190-day gestation period, the female bears a single offspring. When the baby is born, it immediately attaches itself to its mother's fur, where it blends in well with its mother and is difficult to detect. The mother will feed the baby for six months, and the baby will cling to its mother during that time, although it can walk after one month. Young ant-eaters will stay with their mother up to two years. The anteater is usually silent, but the baby will whistle shrilly when left alone.

The main predators for this mammal are jaguars, pumas, and other big cats. It does use its strong front legs and long claws for defense.

Giant Anteater

EDENTATA • MYRMECOPHAGIDAE
MYRMECOPHAGA TRIDACTYLA

WEIGHT: 17.5 to 50.5 pounds (8 to 23 kg)

LENGTH: 40 to 50 inches (100 to 130 cm)

LIFE SPAN: 26 years

SPECIAL DESIGN FEATURE: The giant anteater has very long claws for digging into termite and ant hills. They also have a very long sticky tongue for extracting the termites.

DID YOU KNOW? The giant anteater's sense of smell is 40 times stronger than man's.

Giant Panda

The giant panda is a very beautiful and rare animal. The panda is found in the bamboo forests of south central China. Its distinctive coat is white with black markings around its eyes, ears, and front and back legs.

The canine teeth of the panda are pointed like a lion. However, the panda prefers a diet mainly of bamboo instead of meat. Its teeth are designed to chew and crush the thick bamboo, and it can chew more than 3,000 bamboo stalks in one day.

Pandas are very flexible so that they can do amazing twists and turns. They even do somersaults. They were designed with a special wrist bone to keep bamboo stalks in their fingers.

Pandas are generally solitary and do not hibernate in the winter but continue to forage the forest for food. They do not mind the snow at all and have even been observed playing in it.

Babies are born between July and September, most often in a hollow tree. As many as two babies are born, but generally only one survives. They are very tiny when born but grow rapidly. Baby pandas cannot run, climb trees, or eat bamboo until they are about 7 months old. They will stay with their mother until they are 18 to 20 months old.

The panda's enemies include leopards and wild dogs. Pandas have very powerful jaws and teeth which they use to protect their young.

The estimated panda population is fewer than 1,500. Farming and housing have replaced much of its original habitat. Also endangering their population is the bamboo plant itself. From time to time, certain types of bamboo will flower and die, leaving no bamboo for the panda. This has caused many pandas to die of starvation.

Pandas do not survive well in captivity. The first pandas to be shipped to zoos lived only four or five years and died without producing any offspring. It is still rare to see a panda in a zoo and even more rare to see a baby panda.

Giant Panda

CARNIVORA • PROCYONIDAE
AILUROPODA MELANOLEUCA
HEIGHT: 6 feet (1.8 m)
WEIGHT: 200 pounds (90 kg)
LENGTH: 5 feet (150 cm)
LIFE SPAN: 20 years
SPECIAL DESIGN FEATURE: Pandas have a very special wrist bone to help keep the bamboo in their fingers.
DID YOU KNOW? Pandas can chew on more than 3,000 bamboo sticks in one day.

Giraffe

The giraffe is the tallest of all land animals. Its heart can be over two feet long and is engineered with a network of bypasses and anti-pooling valves that allow the giraffe to raise and lower its 500-pound (227 kg) neck and head without fainting. NASA scientists have studied the giraffe's uniquely created anatomy to help them develop gravity suits.

A giraffe has only seven vertebrae in its neck, as do all mammals. The neck was designed so this animal could feed from the high branches of trees. Giraffes have a unique pattern of spots. No two are the same.

All giraffes have outgrowths of bone on their heads, called ossicones, that look like horns. Even baby giraffes have them. When the baby is born, the horns are gristle and lie flat, but as the giraffe matures, the horns turn to bone and are covered with hair.

Giraffes are herbivores and feed on leaves and buds of trees, their favorite being the acacia. Females feed on the lower branches while the males reach the higher ones. They have a tongue that extends their reach by as much as 20 inches (51 cm). Like the cow, a giraffe has no incisors on its upper jaw, but has a pad that it uses to bite and tear. It does have jaw teeth that it uses to chew its cud like a cow.

Social animals that travel in herds ranging from 2 to 40, giraffes have excellent eyesight and hearing. They have few enemies; however, lions will attack babies and even some adults. Giraffes can be a poor choice for a lion's meal, since they have been known to kick the head off of a lion with their powerful hind kick.

The giraffe is silent most of the time but can make a wide variety of sounds, including mooing, bleating, bellowing, snoring, whistling, grunting, and coughing.

The giraffe's gestation period is 15 months and she gives birth in a special area designated for calving. Most baby animals are born head first. Since the mother giraffe gives birth standing up, her calf is born rear end first. This protects the baby's head and neck from hitting the ground and breaking as it is born. Within an hour the calf is able to wobble about and may even run a short distance. The calf stands about six feet tall (2 m) and weighs 150 pounds (68 kg) at birth.

Man is the only threat to the giraffe. It is hunted still for food although it is against the law. Giraffes have long been a favorite in zoos around the world and have been given as rare and valuable gifts from one king to another in Europe and Asia.

Giraffe

ARTIODACTYLA • GIRAFFADAE
GIRAFFA CAMELOPARDARLIS
HEIGHT: 18 feet (5.5 m)
WEIGHT: 1,765 to 4,200 pounds (801–1,905 kg)
LIFE SPAN: 25 years
SPECIAL DESIGN FEATURE: The giraffe has a large heart to allow it to raise and lower its head without fainting.
DID YOU KNOW? The giraffe has the same number of vertebrae in its neck (seven) as humans do.

Gorilla

Undiscovered by Europeans until the 19th century, the gorilla is the largest member of the apes. Usually a peaceful giant, a male gorilla can have the strength of six to eight men, and its extraordinary strength makes it fearless. There are two species of gorilla, the mountain gorilla, which has longer fur, and the lowland gorilla.

The gorilla ranges from brown to black with gray mixed in. Mature males have a sagittal crest on their heads and are larger than the females. The face of the gorilla is black and hairless. The gorilla is a quadruped, walking on its knuckles and rarely standing. Males pound their chest when threatened or curious. Young gorillas pound their chest when playing.

Gorillas live in family groups as small as 10 and as large as 30, led by a mature male. These males will often have silver hair on their backs, thus earning them the name "silver back."

Gorillas build a nest every night. They wake up late and go to sleep early.

When not feeding, they like to lie around and groom each other. Gorillas feed on fruit, leaves, bamboo, buds, stems, and other plants. If a gorilla is thirsty, it puts the back of its hand in the water and sucks the water from its coarse hair. It also obtains water from the plants that it eats. Gorillas don't like rivers and avoid crossing even a small stream.

Gorillas mate all year long. The female produces one offspring after a gestation period of nine months. At birth, a gorilla baby weighs four to five pounds but matures quickly. The baby stays with its mother for about three years. These young gorillas like to play with others of the troop, including patient adult males. The female of the species matures at six or seven years while the male matures a year or two later. He will not reach his full size until he is 12 to 14 years old.

Gorillas are a favorite at zoos all over the world. Although they have no natural enemies, they have been hunted and captured by man. In 1960 there were 15,000 gorillas, but today there are fewer than 500.

Gorilla

PRIMATES • PONGIDAE • GORILLA GORILLA

HEIGHT: 6.7 feet (2 m)

WEIGHT: 500 pounds (250 kg)

LIFE SPAN: 50 years

SPECIAL DESIGN FEATURE: The gorilla was created with a thumb on its feet for grasping and climbing.

DID YOU KNOW? The gorilla is the largest member of the ape family and has the strength of six to eight men.

Grizzly Bear

No animal in North America is more respected, feared, or more dangerous than the grizzly bear. Ranging in color from near black and brown to blond and almost white, grizzlies may appear clumsy. Despite their huge mass of bone, muscle, and teeth, they can outrun a horse for short distances. When angry, they are nearly unstoppable.

The grizzly can survive quite well on the treeless tundra, but prefers woodlands and forests with open grassy patches. While omnivorous, the grizzly is essentially a vegetarian. It uses its long claws to dig for bulbs, roots, and rodents, and is also fond of grass and honey. Grizzlies usually eat wounded or weak animals, although they have been known to kill large animals such as caribou, moose, and sometimes livestock.

In the fall, they gorge themselves and settle in a den until the following spring, falling into a deep sleep called torpor. This is not a true hibernation.

Grizzlies mark their territory by clawing trees. One bear's range can be up to ten square miles. Grizzlies are solitary but will tolerate one another. Too big to risk injury, they stare each other down, growl, snap their teeth, and use strong body language as a warning. During salmon runs, great numbers of bears will gather and share fishing spots. If a large dominant bear appears, the smaller bears move. When startled, wounded, feeding, or with its cubs, the grizzly bear can explode in fury and attack with unbelievable speed and power. No other animal is so unpredictable in temperament.

The female grizzly usually gives birth to two cubs inside her winter den. The babies are only eight inches (20 cm) long, blind, with little hair and no teeth. The cubs stay with their mother one or two winters before they are on their own. Male grizzlies will sometimes kill cubs, but the mother grizzly will fight fiercely, willing to give her life for her cubs.

The grizzly has no enemies other than man. Indians used the claws and teeth of the grizzly for necklaces, grizzly hide for blankets, the meat for food, the bones for tools, and the skull as a trophy. Early settlers in America found the grizzly as far east as Ohio, and grizzlies on the Plains once followed the thousands of buffalo herds across America. Regulated bear hunting has helped increase the bear population in Alaska. Since male bears sometimes kill cubs, hunters harvesting the adult male allows more young to survive to adulthood.

Grizzly Bear

CARNIVORA • URSIDAE
URSUS ARCTOS HORRIBILIS
HEIGHT: 6 feet (1.8 m) (standing)
WEIGHT: 500–1,200 pounds (227–545 kg)
LENGTH: 6 to 10 feet (1.8–3 m)
LIFE SPAN: 30 years
SPECIAL DESIGN FEATURE: The grizzly bear has an excellent sense of smell. They can smell carrion up to 18 miles (29 km) away.
DID YOU KNOW? The grizzly bear is mainly a vegetarian.

Hippopotamus

The hippopotamus is the third heaviest animal in the world (the first being the elephant and the second the rhinoceros). Hippos live in western, central, eastern, and southern Africa.

The hippopotamus may look like a friendly giant with a built-in smile, but it is actually very dangerous and can kill animals with a single bite. The hippo has fierce-looking teeth which are used for eating grasses, roots, large reeds, and aquatic plants. The lower canines can grow to be 20 inches (51 cm) long, 13 inches (33 cm) longer than the tooth of *Tyrannosaurus rex*. Hippos eat as much as 90 pounds (41 kg) of food a day. At night, they come out of the water to feed on the land. During the day, they spend up to 18 hours in a lake or river, shielding themselves from the hot African sun.

The skin of the hippo is five inches (13 cm) thick. The skin secretes a pinkish fluid that oozes over the hippo's body and protects it from the scorching sun. The hippo is hairless except for the tips of the ears and the muzzle.

Very graceful in the water, hippos tuck their front legs in and paddle with their hind feet. Their eyes, nose, and ears are on the top of the head, allowing them to stay nearly submerged and still know what is going on. When the hippo dives, it presses its short ears against its head and closes its nostrils. It can stay underwater for over five minutes. Hippos also like to wallow in mud like pigs. Hippos share the water with crocodiles. Most crocodiles leave baby hippos alone because a protective mother can, and will, bite crocodiles in two if provoked.

The hippopotamus is very social, living in groups ranging from 15 to 20. One dominant male will reign over the group for as long as ten years. Other males stay in bachelor groups until bold enough to challenge the leader.

After a gestation period of eight months, the hippopotamus has a single calf, born during the rainy season. Sometimes the baby is born underwater and must surface quickly to take its first breath. It usually nurses underwater for about five months. A baby will stay with its mother for several years, and often several youngsters are seen following a single female. Female hippos will take turns watching the young while the others feed.

Hippos can be very dangerous. They have fatally injured people while attacking boats. Hippos often overgraze an area, which can cause severe soil erosion. This results in the removal of the hippos by organized hunting.

Hippopotamus

ARTIODACTYLA • HIPPOPOTAMIDAE
HIPPOPOTAMUS AMPHIBIUS
HEIGHT: 5 feet (1.5 m)
WEIGHT: 5,525 pounds (2,500 kg)
LENGTH: 14–15 feet (4–5 m)
LIFE SPAN: 45 years
SPECIAL DESIGN FEATURE: The hippopotamus's eyes, nose, and ears are on top of its head. They can close their nose and ears and comfortably dive in the water.
DID YOU KNOW? The skin of the hippo is five inches (13 cm) thick and the skin secretes a pinkish fluid to protect it from the sun.

Koala

Often called a bear, the koala is, in fact, a marsupial with a backward-facing pouch. In the wild, this animal is rarely seen because it lives high in the tops of trees. Even though it is arboreal, the koala will occasionally venture to the ground where it can be easy prey for dogs.

The fur on its back is so thick that the koala is virtually waterproof, and it has special thumbs that help it feed. The male is about twice the size of the female.

Koalas sleep about 20 hours a day and spend the rest of their time eating. Picky eaters, koalas eat only the leaves of a few species of eucalyptus, from which they obtain most of their water. They also have been seen drinking dew off of the ground.

Koalas move slowly to conserve energy. However, they can move quickly and leap from one tree to another. A tame koala will cling to whomever is holding it, but in the wild, they will bite, kick, and claw with vigor until free.

The male matures at five years. He has a special gland on his chest that leaves a scent on the tree he occupies. This scent, along with his occasional bellow, will hopefully attract a mate. A female can breed at two years of age.

Like all marsupials, the baby koala is born bean-sized and finds its way into its mother's pouch. Once it attaches to its mother's nipple, it does not venture out until fully developed, about 13 weeks.

The mother carries the baby in her pouch for up to six months and then allows the youngster to cling to her back or stomach for another two to three months. When the young koala is old enough for something other than milk, it will eat partially digested leaves (called pap) found in its mother's droppings.

Koalas were almost hunted to extinction because of the demand for their fur, but they are now protected. Many of them are displayed in zoos, and these captive animals are the most photographed creatures in Australia.

Koala

MARSUPIALIA • PHASCOLARCTIDAE
PHASCOLARCTOS CINEREUS

WEIGHT: 33 pounds (15 kg)

LENGTH: 2-3 feet (60–90 cm)

LIFE SPAN: 10–15 years

SPECIAL DESIGN FEATURE: The koala's thumbs are specially designed to help them feed and grasp.

DID YOU KNOW? The koalas get most of their water from eating eucalyptus leaves.

Leopard

Leopards can jump the highest and the farthest of the terrestrial land mammals. Humans rarely see leopards because their markings blend into their environment. Their color and the length of their fur vary depending on the climate. The leopard is tawny yellow, white underneath, and has black spots on most of its body.

Solitary cats, leopards have excellent hearing and eyesight and can see at night six times better than humans can. This aids them in their nocturnal hunting.

Leopards often wait in trees for prey, but they can also silently stalk to within a few feet and attack. They feed on deer, birds, monkeys, antelopes, domestic livestock, and sometimes humans. When they make a kill, they'll drag it up a tree to protect it from other predators.

Leopards are able to adapt very well to a variety of habitats including forests, swamps, grasslands, and mountainous regions. They live in Africa, south of the Sahara, and southern Asia.

The males are generally larger than the females. Leopards, like all members of the cat family, mark their territory by urinating and scratching the bark on certain trees in their range.

After a gestation period of three months, a female usually bears between two and four cubs. While the cubs are small, the mother will carry them to a new hiding place every few days to help keep them from harm. They will stay with their mother for about two years.

Leopards have been hunted for years for their beautiful coat. In the 1960s, nearly 50,000 leopards were killed. Today the leopard is protected, but it is hunted still because of its attacks on livestock. However, farmers have recognized the leopard's usefulness in controlling some pests such as baboons, bush pigs, and rats, which do great damage to crops.

Leopard

CARNIVORA • FELIDAE • PANTHERA PARDAS

WEIGHT: 80–100 pounds (36–45 kg)

LENGTH: 8 feet (2.5 m)

LIFE SPAN: 12 years

SPECIAL DESIGN FEATURE: The leopard has excellent hearing and eyesight. They can see six times better than humans at night.

DID YOU KNOW? Leopards can jump the highest of all the land animals — 18 feet (5.5 m)!

Lion

Known as the "king of the Jungle," the lion is a symbol of strength and is mentioned in the Bible at least 154 times. Jesus is called the "lion of the tribe of Juda," symbolizing His strength, and one of the most-recognized stories in the Old Testament is Daniel in the lion's den. Lions once inhabited Europe, southern Asia, central India, and all of Africa. The common perception of the lion is that of the male with his long, dark or light-colored mane.

Unlike most big cats, lions live in "prides," numbering as many as 30 animals. They prefer the open plains as opposed to other cats, which mostly live in forests and swamps. A pride includes one or more males and a number of lionesses with their young. The males also form bachelor groups. Lions spend the day in the shade and sleep up to 18 hours.

When hunting, a lion can run a short distance at 40 miles (64 km) per hour, leap 40 feet (12 m), and jump 12 feet (3.7 m) high. These cats hunt at dusk, but the lionesses do most of the work. They surround the prey and drive it downwind to a trap set by the other lionesses. The male lion gets first choice of the kill even though he had no part in bringing it down. After gorging himself, he will allow the others to eat what remains.

Lions are mainly carnivorous and kill only what they can eat. They get their vitamins from the entrails of the herbivores they kill and will eat anything from mice to elephants. If a lion is hungry enough, it will attack larger animals, risking death.

Female lions have cubs every two years. Before birth, she selects a hiding place safe from predators, sheltered, and close to water. After a gestation period of about 107 days, a lioness gives birth to between two and five cubs. For the first 2 months of their lives, they drink only their mother's milk. At six weeks of age, they begin to accompany their mother hunting and acquire a taste for meat. They follow their mother for up to 15 months and learn to hunt and capture small prey. After two years, when their mother is pregnant again, the cubs are forced to leave her.

Man has hunted the lion for centuries. The lion is protected by law in many countries. The lion was a favorite animal of the ancient Assyrians and Babylonians and continues to be a favorite zoo animal today.

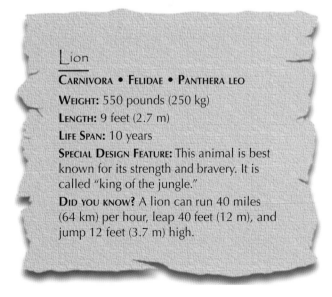

Lion

CARNIVORA • FELIDAE • PANTHERA LEO

WEIGHT: 550 pounds (250 kg)

LENGTH: 9 feet (2.7 m)

LIFE SPAN: 10 years

SPECIAL DESIGN FEATURE: This animal is best known for its strength and bravery. It is called "king of the jungle."

DID YOU KNOW? A lion can run 40 miles (64 km) per hour, leap 40 feet (12 m), and jump 12 feet (3.7 m) high.

Moose

The moose is the largest member of the deer family. They live in the forests, tundra, and marshlands of Europe, North America, and Asia.

The moose is dark brown. The back slopes down because of the huge shoulder muscles needed to support its enormous head and antlers. Under the neck of the bull is a dewlap of skin that sways as the moose moves. This is called the bell. Moose have keen hearing, excellent smell, and average eyesight. The long legs are like stilts in water and deep snow. The huge feet steady the enormous body in water, mud, snow, and frozen ground.

Males grow huge palmated antlers (not horns) which are shed after the winter rut. The new antlers start to grow immediately and can have 18 to 20 points. By fall, the antlers are hard, and the moose is ready to spar with other males for the right to mate with nearby cows. They are very vocal and bellow during the breeding season. During the mating season bulls can be very dangerous, and it does not take much to get them angry.

Moose love the water and feed on aquatic plants. They eat water lilies, duckweed, and reeds. In the winter, moose browse in marshy forests and tundra, feeding on trees and plants.

Moose are solitary for the most part but sometimes form small groups. The moose may live out its entire life on 500 to 1,000 acres. Moose can run for miles and have been clocked at 35 miles (56 km) per hour trotting. In full gallop on easy terrain, they can run 45 miles (72 km) per hour. Swift water doesn't matter to a moose. They simply plunge in and swim.

A cow moose has one calf (sometimes two) after a gestation period of eight to nine months. The mother keeps her calf hidden for about ten days until it can safely follow her. Baby moose look very much out of proportion with their long shaky legs. They are red-brown, weighing about 25 pounds (11 kg). They can be easy targets for wolves, bear, and lynx. The young mature in two to three years.

Moose were very important to the early settlers and explorers as a major addition to their winter food supply. Today, thousands of pounds of moose meat are harvested annually. Outfitting and guiding businesses have also made the moose a very important part of the North Country, where trophy hunting is a major sport. Because of the vast area that the moose inhabits, its population is surveyed regularly. Present population estimates are 300,000 to 500,000.

Moose

ARTIODACTYLA • CERVIDAE • ALCES ALCES

HEIGHT: 8 feet (2.4 m) at the shoulders

WEIGHT: 1,315 pounds (595 kg)

LENGTH: 10 feet (3 m)

LIFE SPAN: 20 years

SPECIAL DESIGN FEATURE: The long legs of the moose are like stilts in the water and deep snow. Its huge feet steady its enormous body in mud, snow, and water.

DID YOU KNOW? The moose is the largest member of the deer family.

Platypus

One of the strangest animals that God created was the platypus. It lives in eastern Australia near waterways.

The platypus spends much of its time in the water. The platypus has brown, beaver-like fur which water can't penetrate. Twisting this way and that, it uses its beaver-shaped tail, which is also covered with fur, as a rudder. The tail is also used to store body fat. The back feet are used for steering and the front for propelling.

The adult male platypus is three times larger than the female and has poisonous spurs on its hind legs. It is thought that this spur is used in the springtime breeding season in territorial disputes. The platypus has five toes on each of its webbed front and back feet. When the platypus walks, it folds back the web on its front feet to reveal its claws, giving it a better grip.

In the early morning and late afternoon, the platypus leaves its burrow to feed on small water animals such as worms, shrimp, and insect larvae. It finds its prey by sensors in its leathery duck-like beak. It surfaces often to breathe and to chew its meals.

The platypus is a monotreme. The female lays two small eggs and incubates them between her tail and abdomen for approximately two weeks. Unlike most mammals, the female platypus has no nipples. The babies feed on milk that oozes onto the mother's abdomen. The young are weaned between four and five months of age.

Platypus fossils have been found in Australia, and a fossilized platypus tooth was found in South America in 1991. When the first platypus arrived in England in the 1700s, the scientists who examined the specimen thought it was a fraud. In fact, they thought a taxidermist took the parts from several animals and mounted them on a body of another animal. However, the platypus is real and a marvelous creation.

Platypus

MONOTREMATA • ORNITHORHYNCHIDAE
ORNITHORHYNCHUS ANATINUS

WEIGHT: 4-1/2 pounds (2 kg)
LENGTH: 21–22 inches (55 cm)
LIFE SPAN: 10 years
SPECIAL DESIGN FEATURE: The platypus was created with sensors in its leathery duck-like beak to find its food.
DID YOU KNOW? The platypus is a monotreme or egg-laying mammal.

Polar Bear

Largest of all the bear species, the beautiful polar bear is the king of the bears. They live on the southern edge of the Arctic ice cap and are specially equipped for their arctic lifestyle.

The polar bear's coat ranges from white to ivory. Individual hairs are hollow and act as a heat conductor to help insulate the body. A polar bear can sleep comfortably in conditions that would kill a human in minutes. The white color of the coat acts like a camouflage on the ice and allows the bear to stalk its prey, but under the fur, the skin is black. Polar bears also have fur on the soles of their feet to keep them from slipping on ice.

The polar bear is the best swimmer of all the bears. It has been observed swimming over 50 miles (80 km) at 6 miles (10 km) per hour without rest, and can swim underwater for up to two minutes. Its forepaws are webbed and designed for swimming and the hind feet act like rudders for steering.

The main food source for the polar bear is seals. It stalks the seals both in and out of the icy cold water. Of all bears, the polar bear is the most carnivorous. In fact, this nomadic giant is believed to be the largest land carnivore in the world. Its diet also includes crabs, rodents, hares, caribou, fish, and plants such as berries when in season. When hunting, the polar bear patrols coastal waters and uses its keen eyesight and hearing and excellent sense of smell. It can detect the smell of seals, dead whales, and carrion up to 20 miles (32 km) away. The polar bear is also an intelligent animal. It is worth mentioning that at the polar bear exhibit at the Australia Zoo, they list the polar bear's diet, which includes a variety of food (mainly plants).

Polar bears are solitary for the most part, but they occasionally come together and feed. Sometimes they follow each other for miles. When they meet, they sniff noses and may play and wrestle. Sometimes they show aggressive behavior.

Usually two cubs are born in November or December. They are very small like all other species of bears, weighing one to two pounds (0.5–1 kg). In March or April they leave the den with their mother to explore their surroundings. They stay with their mother until the spring of their third year, learning all they need to know to survive in their habitat.

Hunting of the polar bear did not start until the 17th century. Polar bears were hunted for their beautiful white coat, but now they are protected and hunting is regulated. The present population is an estimated 40,000.

Polar Bear

CARNIVORA • URSIDAE • URSUS MARITIMUS

HEIGHT: 5 feet (1.5 m) at shoulders, 8–11 feet (2.5–3.4 m) standing

WEIGHT: 650–1,700 pounds (295–790 kg)

LENGTH: 6-l/2–8 feet (2–2.5 m)

LIFE SPAN: 20–25 years

SPECIAL DESIGN FEATURE: The hairs of the polar bear's coat insulate the body from the cold temperatures and act as a heat conductor.

DID YOU KNOW? The polar bear is a very good swimmer and can swim over 50 miles (80 km).

Porcupine

Over 25,000 sharp pointed quills cover the porcupine's body, protecting this slow-moving animal from its enemies. The barbed quills are loosely attached to the skin and can grow up to three inches long. Many inexperienced predators have learned the hard way and have suffered and died because of the porcupine's quills.

The coat of a porcupine is brown with white hair mixed in. The quills are black and yellow. Porcupines' bright-orange teeth gnaw and eat wooden handles of tools, shoes, gloves, steering wheels, canoe paddles, and even glass. Their main food is bark and conifer needles in the winter and a variety of plants, grass, berries, and small shoots in the summer. They also like to gnaw on shed antler.

Mainly nocturnal, porcupines prefer mixed forest areas, but sometimes their habitat includes open tundra and pastures. Their well-designed claws and feet help them balance themselves well. They are excellent climbers, observed as high as 20 feet (6 m) up a tree. They den on the ground in logs or rock crevices. There may be several dens with well-worn trails leading back and forth.

Porcupines rely on their keen hearing and excellent sense of smell for survival but have poor eyesight. A threatened porcupine bristles up its back and lashes repeatedly with its tail at its enemy. If the predator attacks, it receives a nose and mouth full of sharp quills. The barbs keep working deeper into the animal's skin. The predator can starve or die of infection if they can't free themselves from the quills.

There are few predators who have learned to flip the porcupine on its back and attack the soft stomach that is free of quills. The fisher, along with the wolverine and cougar, are a few of the porcupine's predators.

After mating in the fall, porcupines bear a single baby in the spring. The baby is weaned in about four weeks and fully mature at 18 to 30 months.

A misleading concept regarding the porcupine is that it can throw its quills. It cannot. Some porcupines are hunted by man for meat.

Porcupine

RODENTIA • ERETHIZONTIDAE
ERETHIZON DORSATUM
WEIGHT: 40 pounds (18 kg)
LENGTH: 28 inches (70 cm)
LIFE SPAN: 15–17 years
SPECIAL DESIGN FEATURE: The porcupine is covered with over 25,000 sharp, pointed quills on its body.
DID YOU KNOW? Porcupines are excellent tree climbers with very well-designed claws and feet.

Pronghorn Antelope

Designed to run, the pronghorn is the fastest animal in North America and probably the fastest long-distance runner in the world. They can cruise comfortably at 35 miles (56 km) per hour for several miles without tiring. At full speed, they can hit 55 miles (89 km) per hour and leap 20 feet (6 m). It has an extra large heart, windpipe, and lungs to accommodate such speed. They also have extra large front feet with padding to absorb shock. Even though they sometimes run on rough terrain, they seldom show any sign of lameness.

A very handsome animal with reddish tan hair on the back of its neck and back, the pronghorn has white on its belly and rump and a stripe of white across its neck. Both sexes have black horns, which are not antlers. The horns are made up of keratin hairs similar to a rhinoceros horn, and consist of an outer shell, which is shed yearly. The horns range in size from 13 to 20 inches (33–51 cm).

The pronghorn can adjust its body temperature by raising and lowering its hollow hairs. Lowering the hair keeps cold air out; raising it allows air to circulate and body heat to escape.

Only two barriers dictate the pronghorn's territory — forests and badlands. Pronghorns favor lower elevations but can be found as high as 8,000 feet (2.4 km).

Pronghorns search with their phenomenal eyes, scan with their ears, and smell for danger. They live in herds numbering as many as several hundred animals. With this many eyes watching, they have few problems with predators. Some predators of the pronghorn are coyotes and bears.

Pronghorns browse on sage, bitter brush, salt brush, and weeds such as dandelion, thistle, clover, and a variety of others. They can go several days without water because the plants in their diet provide it. They do drink freely when water is available but are very cautious about where they drink. They prefer their watering hole to be out in the open with no high brush where predators can hide. During the heat of the day, they rest and chew their cud.

During mating season, bucks become territorial and will duel over does. The doe has a gestation period of about 250 days and usually gives birth to twins. After only a few days, the fawns can run 20 miles (32 km) per hour and join the herd.

The pronghorns aren't really antelopes, but a separate family made up of just pronghorns, found only on the North American continent. Early explorers called them that because they looked like some of the antelopes found in Africa and other places.

Pronghorn Antelope

ARTIODACTYLA • ANTILOPINAE
ANTILOCAPRA AMERICANA

HEIGHT: 2.6–3.3 feet (80–100 cm)

WEIGHT: 77–155 pounds (35–70 kg)

LENGTH: 4.6 feet (1.4 m)

LIFE SPAN: 15 years

SPECIAL DESIGN FEATURE: The pronghorn is specially designed for running and they are probably the fastest long distance runner in the world.

DID YOU KNOW? The pronghorn antelope has very good eyesight and lives in herds of 20 to hundreds of animals.

Raccoon

The raccoon is one of the most easily recognized wild mammals in North America, with its grayish-brown fur, black mask-like markings around its face, and dark rings around its tail. The territory of the raccoon extends over most of the United States and into southern Canada.

One of the reasons for the raccoon's success is its adaptability to different environments (forests, streams, towns, cities, etc.) Another important factor is the variety of food it eats. It eats crayfish, frogs, snakes, mollusks, mice, shrews, insects, earthworms, turtle eggs, bird eggs (even young birds), berries, nuts, and grains when they are available.

Raccoons prefer their food moist and will often "wash" it in water before eating. They also have clever little hands that they use to handle their food.

Raccoons eat more during the fall in order to develop an inch-thick (2.5 cm) layer of fat on their body. This fatty layer helps sustain them during the winter. They do not hibernate but hole up and sleep for several days in bad weather. The raccoon's fur thins out during the spring and summer.

The mating season for the raccoon is late February or March, and the gestation period is about 60 days. Raccoons have litters of four to seven kits. The young kits remain in their den for eight to ten weeks, feeding on their mother's milk. Afterward, they join their mother on her nightly hunting excursions. They learn how to hunt and the ways of survival. They stay with their mother through the coming winter and leave in the spring.

Raccoons can be viewed as pests when they raid garbage cans, farmers' fields, or chicken houses in the middle of the night. They have long been hunted for their fur. Early settlers even used "coonskins" as currency, and Daniel Boone, Davy Crockett, and Johnny Appleseed were famous for their coonskin caps.

Raccoon

CARNIVORA • PROCYONIDAE • PROCYON LOTOR

WEIGHT: 10–25 pounds (4.5–11 kg)

LENGTH: 16–24 inches (40–60 cm), tail 8–16 inches (20–40 cm)

LIFE SPAN: 10 years

SPECIAL DESIGN FEATURE: The raccoon can successfully adapt to different environments and also a variety of food sources.

DID YOU KNOW? The raccoon does not wash its food to get it clean but rather they prefer their food moist.

Red Kangaroo

The red kangaroo is the largest marsupial. It lives exclusively throughout inland Australia in grasslands, shrublands, and salt pans. Both sexes have black markings on the side of their muzzles. The male is red and is referred to as a "boomer," and the female is called "blue flier." The young are bluish-gray.

Kangaroos have long hind legs and feet and a long, thick, tapered tail. Strong tendons in the hind legs allow the kangaroo to jump 6 to 8 feet (1.8–2.4 m) high and leap distances of 12 to 14 feet (3.7–4.3 m). It can reach speeds up to 35–40 miles (56–64 km) per hour for short distances, but its normal pace is around 8 miles (13 km) per hour.

The forearms of the kangaroo have little fur on them and carry blood vessels close to the surface of the skin. In very hot weather, kangaroos lick their forearms to cool themselves. They also pant to get rid of excess heat.

Red kangaroos live in groups called mobs. Each mob is made up of 100 or more kangaroos and is led by the dominant male. Mainly nocturnal, kangaroos eat grass and short green plants. They like to live near a water supply but can go long periods without water if necessary.

Males fighting for dominance use their forearms to box one another. They balance with their tails and kick with their hind feet, and are capable of ripping open flesh. The kick can be so hard it can actually debowl their enemy. Most times, they are peaceful and would rather hop away than fight. They have few enemies except the dingo and man.

A female kangaroo is fertile throughout the entire year. Gestation is little more than a month. When the young kangaroo, called a joey, is born, it is very tiny (bean size) and weighs only about l/35 of an ounce (0.9 g). It crawls inside its mother's pouch and attaches itself to a nipple to nurse. It will stay there for about eight months before venturing out. By this time, it weighs around seven pounds (3 kg) and will continue to nurse for another six months. The mother often has more than one baby in the pouch at a time — an older one that goes in and out and a younger baby still attached to a nipple. Older joeys need fat-rich milk while the infants need more carbohydrates. In order to fulfill these nutritional needs, God created the mother to be able to produce two types of milk at the same time.

The red kangaroo is considered a pest by farmers because of the other farm animals having to compete for the grasslands. It is nearly impossible to build a fence that will keep the kangaroos out.

Red Kangaroo

MARSUPIALIAM • MACROPODIDAE • MACROPUS RUFUS

HEIGHT: 5 feet (1.5 m)

WEIGHT: 180 pounds (82 kg)

LENGTH: 65 inches (165 cm)

LIFE SPAN: 12–18 years

SPECIAL DESIGN FEATURE: The mother can produce two different kinds of milk to meet the needs of more than one baby. A joey that is still nursing but has left the pouch gets fat-rich milk and the smaller baby gets more carbohydrates in its milk.

DID YOU KNOW? The red kangaroo is the largest living marsupial.

Striped Skunk

Skunks are mostly known for their horrible odor, which is produced by a highly developed anal gland. It is used to deter their enemies. Most of the time a skunk will not discharge its foul scent unless it feels threatened. In fact, they are docile.

A striped skunk has black fur with two white stripes running down its back. Also called a polecat, it is about the size of a domesticated cat. Sometimes several families of skunk will live together. Some skunks will dig their own burrows, while others share burrows dug by other animals, such as raccoons, woodchucks, or foxes. Skunks are also found under buildings, logs, and woodpiles.

The skunk lives in woodlands and grasslands all across the United States and Canada. Mostly nocturnal, it has few enemies except the great horned owl. It is omnivorous, feeding mainly on insects, but its diet also includes mice, frogs, small birds, and eggs. It also uses its long claws to dig up grubs, earthworms, roots, fungi, nuts, and fruit. The skunk hunts its food by scent, sniffing along the ground.

The skunk warns its enemy by pounding its front paws on the ground. If that doesn't work, it turns backwards and sprays a fine mist very accurately up to 12 feet (3.7 m). It can produce this spray up to eight times during an encounter. The spray can cause temporary blindness, and the odor can be detected a half-mile (805 m) away. A predator who is unfortunate enough to be sprayed by the skunk immediately backs off. The offensive scent lingers for weeks as a potent reminder to leave that particular prey alone.

Its mating season runs from February through March. After a gestation period of 50 days, the female has between five to eight babies called kits. The mother will feed her young for about eight weeks until they can hunt for themselves. They stay with their mother until the next mating season and will reach maturity in about 11 months.

Skunks can be a problem for home dwellers in the country or city if they decide to live beneath a building. Many more skunks are hit and killed by cars than are hunted. Skunks carry rabies and can bite and scratch as well as spray.

Striped Skunk

CARNIVORA • MUSTELIDAE • MEPHITUS MEPHITUS

WEIGHT: 2.6–11.7 pounds (1.2–5.3 kg)

LENGTH: 18 inches (45 cm)

LIFE SPAN: 7–9 years

SPECIAL DESIGN FEATURE: The skunk's spray can be very accurate up to 12 feet (3.7 m) away and the skunk can continue to spray up to eight times.

DID YOU KNOW? The skunk lives in burrows that it shares with the animal that actually dug the burrow. They also like to live under buildings, logs, and woodpiles.

Two-toed Sloth

The two-toed sloth is one of the strangest mammals in the world. They spend most of their time hanging upside-down in a tree. There are seven species of sloth divided into two and three-toed varieties. The sloth lives in woodland areas and along riverbanks in areas where the plant "trumpetwood" grows. The two-toed sloth lives from Venezuela to Brazil in South America.

The two-toed sloth is nocturnal and lives in slow motion but is a little more agile than the three-toed. Both move so slow that some people say they can live all their life in the same tree. They hang by means of long, curved claws that resemble meat hooks. Their legs are long, particularly the front legs. The two-toed sloth get their name because they have two claws on the front foot and three on the back foot. Besides using the claws to hang, they can defend themselves by slashing out with their long, curved claws. They can also bite. They have nine teeth on each side of their cheek. These teeth continue to grow throughout their lifetime.

The sloth's head is round and can turn 270 degrees, so it can hold it almost upright while the rest of its body is upside-down. The neck of the two-toed is shorter than the three-toed but is still quite long and flexible. The sloth's eyes and ears are small. The coat of the sloth is dense and coarse, gray-brown in color with white and orange markings on its back. On some species the hair has a greenish tint because of algae growing on it. There is also a moth that lives in its hair.

Details are important to the Creator. God designed the sloth's hair to lie in the opposite direction to that of most mammals allowing rain to run off of its body.

Their diet is trumpetwood leaves and fruit which it locates by smell. They rarely drop to the ground. They do not walk well on the ground but shuffle along dragging themselves with their hands. They can swim well, however.

Their enemies include the jaguar and ocelot. The breeding season is March and April. After a gestation period of 17 to 26 weeks, a single baby is born. The baby immediately attaches itself to its mother and stays there until old enough to leave. There is not a lot of information known about the young. These creatures are very shy and do not come into contact with humans, particularly because it is nocturnal.

Two-toed Sloth

EDENTATA • BRADYPODIDAE
CHOLOEPUS DIDACTYLUS
LENGTH: 21–29 inches (53–74 cm)
WEIGHT: 9 to 20 pounds (4–9 kg)
LIFE SPAN: 20 years
SPECIAL DESIGN FEATURE: The sloth can turn its head 270 degrees so that even when hanging upside-down, the head is almost upright.
DID YOU KNOW? The sloth spends most of its time hanging upside-down in trees, very seldom coming to the ground.

Tiger

The tiger is one of the largest of the big cats. Unlike most cats, tigers love the water and swim very well. They know the water is a good place to find food as well as cool off.

No two tigers have the same pattern of stripes. These markings help them blend into their surroundings, which allow them to move within 30 feet (9 m) of their prey before attacking. Tigers will then charge, dropping their victims with one paw on the shoulder and their teeth at the throat. Once they have their prey on the ground, they break its neck and drag it to a safe place to eat. Tigers bury leftovers to hide them from scavengers. They hunt at night and, while mainly solitary, may occasionally share a kill with another tiger. Their diet consists of deer, rabbit, pig, bear, elk, turtle, fish, and sometimes livestock.

Tigers serve a vital role in animal control. If there were no tigers, some species of deer and other animals would overpopulate, which could lead to disease and starvation.

Tigers mature in three to five years. After a gestation period of three and a half months, a female tiger gives birth to as many as six cubs. Mortality is usually high and only a few of the cubs survive. Born blind and weighing two to three pounds, tiger cubs grow rapidly and can kill for themselves at seven months of age. However, they stay with their mother for two years, learning how to survive.

Tigers are often seen at the circus. However, they are wild animals and can be fatally dangerous. In the wild, human attacks are often by old animals too weak to catch other game or by sick or injured tigers.

Some enemies of the tiger are wild dogs, crocodiles, and man. They are now protected from hunting.

Tigers have been crossed with lions. The offspring are called ligers. When God created the land animals on day 6, He said He created kinds. He then said be fruitful and multiply. There can be changes within the kind, but it stays within the kind. Crossing two members of the cat family always produces cats. I wonder what the first cat looked like.

Tiger

CARNIVORA • FELIDAE • PANTHERA TIGRIS

HEIGHT: 3 feet (1 m)

LENGTH: 9 feet (2.7 m); tail, 3 feet (1 m)

WEIGHT: 400–500 pounds (180–230 kg)

LIFE SPAN: 25 years

SPECIAL DESIGN FEATURE: The tiger has stripes on its body making it practically invisible by blending into the surroundings.

DID YOU KNOW? The tiger is the largest member of the cat family.

Wolverine

The wolverine is the largest member of the weasel family. Its home includes the arctic and subarctic regions of Europe, Asia, and North America.

The stockily built wolverine has very thick, dark brown fur, a white mark on its forehead, and two broad yellowish-white stripes down both sides of its body. It can run, swim, and climb very well. It has powerful short legs with broad paws and long sharp claws. The broad paws are like snowshoes, enabling it to hunt well during the winter.

The wolverine's diet consists of a variety of items such as mice, rats, other small mammals, eggs, birds, berries, and rotting carcasses. In the winter, a wolverine hunts larger game such as caribou, elk, and moose. If it doesn't finish its meal, the wolverine buries the remainder in snow or soil and then covers the carcass with a musk odor that will deter other predators. People living in the wilderness have had the misfortune of having their meat supply ruined by wolverines. The animals break into storage sheds and spray the meat, rendering it useless for humans.

The solitary wolverine lives in evergreen forests, finding shelter wherever it can. Very courageous and fierce, a wolverine can drive a much larger animal, such as a bear, away from a meal. It will face down enemies by baring its teeth, raising its hair, and growling. It uses its strong jaws and teeth to tear meat from bones and crush bones up to two inches (5 cm) in diameter.

The wolverine mating season is during July and August. After eight months, it gives birth to as many as four babies. The young are weaned at eight to ten weeks but stay with their mother for as long as two years, reaching maturity at four.

Eskimos prize the wolverine for its thick fur, which they use to line their parkas.

Wolverine

CARNIVORA • MUSTELIDAE • GULO GULO

WEIGHT: 60 pounds (27 kg)

LENGTH: 4 feet (1.2 m)

LIFE SPAN: 16 years

SPECIAL DESIGN FEATURE: The wolverine has powerful short legs with broad paws and long sharp claws. This enables him to run, swim, and climb very well.

DID YOU KNOW? The wolverine is the largest member of the weasel family and is very courageous and fierce.

Wombat

The wombat is a large, sturdy marsupial that lives in Australia. There are several kinds of wombats, including the Tasmanian wombat, the common wombat, and the hairy-nosed wombat. It is one of the largest burrowing animals in the world.

Wombats are black, brown, gray, or cream. God designed the pouch of the wombat to face backward so that when it burrows into the ground, the pouch does not fill with dirt. The common wombat can grow to the size of a small pig. Predators get a headache if they chase a wombat into its burrow. Since wombats have a hardened pad on their rump, they can use that to crush the head of an attacker against the burrow wall.

Wombats dig long burrows with several entrances, and a colony of wombats may share the same burrow. They are mostly solitary in their habitat and come out at night to feed on vegetation and grasses.

After mating, a female wombat will give birth to a bean-sized baby. The baby then drags itself to the backward-facing pouch, which will be its home for the next six to ten months. The mother cares for her baby another five to ten months after it leaves her pouch.

Wombats are playful and intelligent and make good pets. In captivity they like to curl up on their caretaker's lap and sleep.

Wombat

MARSUPIALA • VOMBATIDAE
VOMBATUS URSINUS

LENGTH: 30 inches (75 cm)
WEIGHT: 40–80 pounds (18–36 kg)
LIFE SPAN: 5–15 years
SPECIAL DESIGN FEATURE: The pouch of this marsupial faces backward so that it doesn't fill with dirt as the wombat burrows.
DID YOU KNOW? The wombat is one of the largest burrowing animals in the world.

Zebra

The Zebra is a wild horse and lives in East Africa. Its habitat is the savannas and open forests, in which it spends the entire day grazing. If the weather in summer is too hot, the zebra will rest during the day and nourish itself at night.

Zebras have a short, stiff mane and tufted tail. Hard, wart-like knobs, called chestnuts, are found only on their front legs. Some evolutionists believe the chestnuts are the remnants of lost toes, but they are actually just calluses, not bones.

Zebras live near watering holes and drink at dawn and dusk. This is a dangerous place since lions, the zebra's chief enemy, often wait there for prey. Zebras usually escape by running from their predators, but if surprised they are easy to kill. Other enemies with which the zebra has to contend are the hyena, cheetah, wild dog, and man.

The male and female of the species mostly live apart. A dominant stallion will control 10 to 15 mares, while young males congregate in their own herds. Combined herds can number as many as several hundred.

Zebra mares give birth after a 370-day gestation period. Long-legged and short-bodied, a zebra newborn weighs 66 to 77 pounds (30–35 kg). Shortly after birth, the foal stands on wobbly legs and instantly tries to nurse. In a short time, it will run with the herd. A newborn zebra's stripes are not fully formed (they are dark brown with white stripes). As they mature, the dark brown darkens to black. No two zebra stripes are exactly the same (an identifier not unlike a human fingerprint).

Because it takes too much time to train them and since they are not as strong as a horse, people have not domesticated the zebra. Zebras have been bred with donkeys, and the offspring are zonkeys. This helps explain the great variety of the horse kind. God created the kinds of animals and there are changes within the kind, but there is a limit, and it doesn't change outside of the kind.

Zebra

PERISSODACTYLA • EQUIDAE
EQUUS ZEBRA ZEBRA

HEIGHT: 3.6–5 feet (1.1–1.5 m) at shoulder

WEIGHT: 546–785 pounds (248–357 kg)

LENGTH: 6.6–7.3 feet (2–2.3 m)

LIFE SPAN: 10 years

SPECIAL DESIGN FEATURE: The zebra's stripes make them difficult to see when they venture out to feed and water at dusk.

DID YOU KNOW? The zebra is a wild horse from Africa. They are one of the true wild horses of the world.

Appendix:
Selected Sketches & Sizes of Footprints*

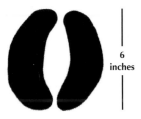

American Bison

6 inches

Beaver (front)

3 inches

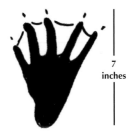

Beaver (hind)

7 inches

Black Rhino

Giant Panda

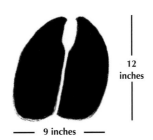

Giraffe

12 inches

9 inches

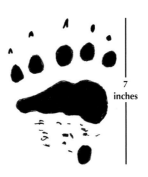

Grizzly Bear (front)

7 inches

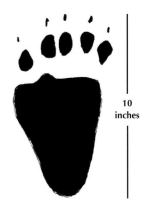

Grizzly Bear (hind)

10 inches

* Not to Scale

Hippopotamus

Kangaroo (front & hind)

Koala (front)

Koala (hind)

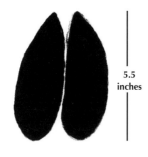

5.5 inches

Moose

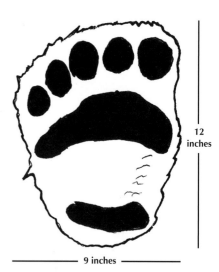

12 inches

9 inches

Polar Bear

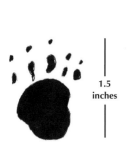

1.5 inches

2.75 inches

Porcupine (front)

Porcupine (hind)

Pronghorn Antelope

Raccoon (front)

Raccoon (hind)

Striped Skunk (front)

Striped Skunk (hind)

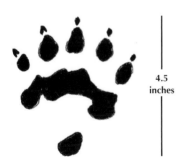

Wolverine (front)

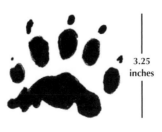

Wolverine (hind)

Zebra

Glossary

ANTLER	a solid horn that falls off and regrows every year.
AQUATIC	living in or near water.
ARBOREAL	living in trees (e.g., monkeys).
BROWSER	an animal that consumes tender shoots, twigs, shrubs, and leaves.
BURROW	a hole in the ground made by an animal for shelter and habitation.
BURROWING	an act of tunneling or digging by an animal.
CAMOUFLAGE	coloration that blends in with the background or environment.
CARNIVORE	an animal that eats other animals.
CARRION	dead and decaying flesh.

CHESTNUT	a callus on the inner side of the leg of a horse.
CUB	a young, meat-eating mammal such as a lion or bear.
DEWLAP	a fold of skin that hangs loosely under the neck of the moose.
DIGIT	a finger or a toe.
ECHOLOCATION	the process of sensing objects by sending out sounds that are reflected back. (Bats use echolocation.)
EMBRYO	an infant not yet born or hatched.
ENDOTHERMIC	warm-blooded.
EXTINCT	no longer existing.
FOREST	a thick growth of trees and underbrush covering a large area.

GESTATION the length of time from conception to birth.

GRAZER an animal that feeds on grass (e.g., cattle).

GREGARIOUS liking companionship, tending to associate with others of one's kind.

HABITAT the place where a particular animal or plant lives, grows, and survives.

HERBIVORE an animal that eats vegetation most of the time.

HIBERNATION a period of time when an animal goes into prolonged inactivity with lowered metabolism. This usually occurs by the onset of cold weather.

HORN a permanent hollow sheath of keratin arising from a bony core anchored to the skull.

INCISOR a tooth for cutting and gnawing.

INCUBATION the method of keeping eggs warm as they develop and hatch.

JOEY a baby kangaroo.

KERATIN a fibrous protein that forms the horn tissue on animals.

KIT a young, fur-bearing animal.

MACROPOD having long legs and large feet (e.g., the kangaroo).

MAMMAL a class of higher vertebrates that feed young with milk secreted by mammary glands.

MARSHLAND an area of land that is soft, wet, and grassy.

MARSUPIAL an order of mammals that has a pouch on its abdomen that contains the milk glands and also carries the young.

MIGRATE to move from one place or area to another.

MOB an Australian term for a group of kangaroos.

MONOTREME an egg-laying mammal which feeds its young milk, but does not have nipples.

NOCTURNAL active mostly at night.

Omnivore an animal that eats both meat and vegetables.

Ossicones the bony-like gristle that grows on the top of the giraffe's head.

Palmated having a shape similar to a hand with fingers extended, (e.g., a moose's antler).

Pap the droppings of the mother koala that consists of partially digested eucalyptus leaves. This is what the young koalas eat when they are old enough for something other than milk, but cannot chew the tough leaves.

Predator an animal that hunts and kills another animal for food.

Prehensile used for grasping by curling around an object.

Pride a group of lions that live together, led by an adult male.

Primates a group of mammals that includes monkeys and apes.

Quadruped an animal that has four feet.

Quill a hollow sharp spine (like those of a porcupine).

Radial a special wrist bone in the panda which is a mass of bone or cartilage in the tendon which helps keep the bamboo in its fingers.

Regurgitate to throw up incompletely digested food.

Ruminate to chew food that has been chewed and swallowed such as a cow chewing their cud.

Rut an annual hormonal stage that male members of the deer family go through prior to and during the mating season.

Rodent the group of gnawing animals which includes mice and rats.

Sagittal the crest on the head of a gorilla that slopes back from their forehead and has a definite ridge.

Savanna a tropical or sub-tropical grassland containing scattered trees.

SCAVENGER an animal that feeds on dead animals that it has not killed (i.e., hyena, wolverine).

SOLITARY being, living, or going alone.

TERRESTRIAL relating to the land as opposed to sea or air.

TORPOR a state of inactivity brought about by cold weather in which the animal's metabolic rate slows and less food reserves are used.

TUNDRA the treeless region of the arctic and subarctic regions having permanetly frozen soil and low-growing vegetation.

UNGULATE having hooves.

Bibliography

American Museum of Natural History, editor. *Illustrated Library of Nature: Animal Traits*, Vol. 1. New York: H.S. Stuttman, Co. Inc., 1971.

Bartoli, Stefania, and Luigi Boitani. *Simon & Schuster's Guide to Mammals*. New York: Simon & Schuster, Inc., 1982.

Bergman, Dr. Jerry. "Mammals Present Some Milky Problems." *Creation Ex Nihilo*, 13(2):39 (March/May 1991).

Biel, Timothy Levi. *Zoobooks — Tigers*. San Diego, CA: Wildlife Education Ltd., 1992.

Bisacre, Michael. *The Illustrated Encyclopedia of Plants & Animals*. Exeter Books, 1979.

Burn, Barbara. *National Audubon Society Collection Nature Series —North American Mammals*. New York, NY: Bonanza Books, 1991.

Burt, William H., and Richard P. Grossenheider. *A Field Guide to the Mammals*. Boston, MA: National Wildlife Federation, Houghton Mifflin Co., 1976.

Burton, Dr. Maurice, and Robert Burton, editors. *Funk & Wagnalls Wildlife Encyclopedia* Vol 1,2,3. New York: B.P.C. Publishing Ltd, 1970).

Carwardine, Mark, and Jim Channell. *Explore the World of Amazing Animals*. Racine, WI: Western Pub. Company, Inc., 1991.

Chapman, Geoff. "The Camel." *Creation Ex Nihilo*, 12(4):28 (Sept/Nov 1990).

Chapman, Geoff. "Weird and Wonderful Koalas." *Creation Ex Nihilo*, 19(4):36 (Sept/Nov 1997).

Chapman, Geoff. "Why Pandas Have Sharp Teeth." *Creation Ex Nihilo*, 19(4):33 (Sept/Nov 1997).

Chinery, Michael. *The Kingfisher Illustrated Encyclopedia of Animals*. New York: Kingfisher Books, Grisewood & Dempsey Inc., 1992.

Dalrymple, Byron W. *North American Game Animals*. New York: Crown Pub., 1978.

Dengate, Heather. *Safari Round the World*. New South Wales, Australia: Western Plains Zoo, Beaver Press, 1993.

Doolan, Robert. "Helpful Animals." *Creation Ex Nihilo*, 17(3):10–13 (June/Aug. 1995).

Doolan, Robert. "How Did the Platypus Get Down Under." *Creation Ex Nihilo*, 13(1):24 (Dec/Feb 1991).

Doolan, Robert, editor. "Platypus Tooth Bites Hard Into Long-held Beliefs." *Creation Ex Nihilo*, 14(1) (Dec/Feb 1992), p. 13.

Doolan, Robert, editor. "The Trouble With Horse Evolution." *Creation Ex Nihilo*, 13(2):39 (March/May 1991).

Doolan et al. "The Platypus? A Freak, a Fraud, and Now a New Finding." *Creation Ex Nihilo*, 8(3):6–9 (June 1986).

Dreves, Denis. "Beavers — Acquatic Architects." *Creation Ex Nihilo*, 14(2):38–41 (March/May 1993).

Elman, Robert. *Bears, Rulers of the Wilderness*. Stamford, CT: Longmeadow Press, 1992.

Haycock, George. *North American Wildlife*. New York: Exeter Books, 1984.

Hofland, Lynn. "Giraffes — Animals That Stand Out in a Crowd." *Creation Ex Nihilo*, 18(4):10–13 (Sept/Nov 1996).

Iwago, Mitsuaki. *Mitsuaki Iwago's Kangaroos*. San Francisco, CA: Chronicle Books, 1992.

Kish, Joe. *The Jonas Technique*, Vol. 2. Lafayette, CO: Jonas Supply Company, 1978.

Legg, Gerald. *Zigzag Factfinders Monster Animals*. England: Zigzag Publishing, 1997.

Morcombe, Michael. *Michael Morcombe's Australian Marsupials & other Native Mammals*. Sydney, Australia: Summit Books, 1978.

Mosby, Henry S., and Robert H. Giles, editors. *Wildlife Management Techniques*. The Wildlife Society. Ann Arbor, MI: Edwards Brothers, Inc., 1969.

Murie, Olaus J. *Animal Tracks — Peterson Field Guide*. Somerville, MA: Houghton Mifflin, 1974.

Myers, Jack, editor. *Nature's Wonderful Family*. Columbus, OH: Highlights, 1971.

Parish, Steve. *Amazing Facts about Australian Mammals*. Queensland, Australia: Steve Parish Publishing, 1997.

Peters, David. *Giants of Land, Sea & Air — Past & Present*. New York: Sierra Club Books and Alfred A. Knopf Publishing, 1986.

Pines, Paula, editor. *Nature in America*. Pleasantville, NY: Reader's Digest, 1991.

Rubins, Joyce. *Wildlife*. Edison, NJ: Chartwell Books, 1994.

Rubins, Joyce. *The Wildlife Year*. Pleasantville, NY: Readers Digest, 1993.

Schneck, Marcus. *Elephants, Gentle Giants of Africa & Asia*. Stamford, CT: Longmeadow Press.

Server, Lee. *Tigers*. Stamford, CT: Longmeadow Press, 1992.

Shreeve, James. *Nature The Other Earthlings*. New York: Macmillan Publ. Co., 1987.

Wernert, Susan J., editor. *North American Wildlife*. Pleasantville, NY: Reader's Digest, 1982.

Weston, Paula. "Camels — Confirmation of Creation." *Creation Ex Nihilo,* 19(4):26–29 (Sept/Nov 1997).

Weston, Paula, and Carl Wieland. "Bears Across the World." *Creation Ex Nihilo,* 29(4):28–31 (Sept/Nov 1998).

Wexo, John Bonnett. *Zoobooks — The Apes*. San Diego, CA: Wildlife Education Ltd., 1981.

Wexo, John Bonnett. *Zoobooks — Bears*. San Diego, CA: Wildlife Education Ltd., 1982.

Wexo, John Bonnett. *Zoobooks — Big Cats*. San Diego, CA: Wildlife Education Ltd., 1981.

Wexo, John Bonnett *Zoobooks — Elephants*. San Diego, CA: Wildlife Education Ltd., 1980.

Wexo, John Bonnett. *Zoobooks — Giant Pandas*. San Diego, CA: Wildlife Education Ltd., 1988.

Wexo, John Bonnett. *Zoobooks — Giraffes*. San Diego, CA: Wildlife Education Ltd., 1980.

Wexo, John Bonnett. *Zoobooks — Rhinos*. San Diego, CA: Wildlife Educational, Ltd., 1983.

Wexo, John Bonnett. *Zoobooks — Wild Horses*. San Diego, CA: Wildlife Education Ltd., 1982.

Wieland, Dr. Carl, editor. "Turtles Always Turtles." *Creation Ex Nihilo,* 29(4):8 (Sept/Nov 1998).

Wildlife Explorer. Stanford, CT: International Masters Publishers, AB, 1998.